DRAG RACING

The Thrill of Racing

NICKI CLAUSEN-GRACE

Rourke
Publishing LLC
Vero Beach, Florida 32964

www.rourkepublishing.com

PHOTO CREDITS: © Library of Congress: page 5; ©David Ferroni: page 6; © Graham Bloomfield: page 7; © JACK BRADEN: page 8; © Chrysler Media: page 8; © Bryan Eastham: page 9; © Scott Scheibelhut: page 10; © GM Racing Photo: page 12, 16, 22; © Todd Taulman: page 11, 12, 21; © Kevin Norris: page 14; © Arlo Abrahamson: page 16; © bsankow: page 17; ©Honda Media: page 18

Edited by Meg Greve

Cover design by Tara Raymo
Interior design by Teri Intzegian

Library of Congress Cataloging-in-Publication Data

Library of Congress Cataloging-in-Publication Data

Clausen-Grace, Nicki.
  Sprint car racing / Nicki Clausen-Grace.
    p. cm. -- (The thrill of racing)
  Includes index.
  ISBN 978-1-60472-377-9
  1. Automobile racing--Juvenile literature. 2. Sprint cars--Juvenile literature. I. Title.
  GV1029.9.S67C53 2009
  796.72--dc22

                    2008011248

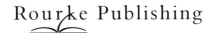

Rourke Publishing

www.rourkepublishing.com – rourke@rourkepublishing.com
Post Office Box 3328. Vero Beach. FL 32964

Table of Contents

Drag Racing

You are sitting in a rumbling machine, wrapped in protective gear, waiting for the Christmas tree light to tell you to drive. You know that winning this short race depends on your **reaction time** and on how well you drive down the track. The light changes, and you step on the gas pedal!

The green bulb on the Christmas tree light tells racers it is time to start.

Almost as soon as you learned how to run, chances are you raced someone to see who was faster. The need to be first is a common **instinct**. Drag racing, a sport where two cars speed down a one-quarter or one-eighth mile (.2 or .4 kilometer) track to see who is fastest, appeals to the desire to finish first.

Thrilling Fact

Heads up racing is when cars start at the same time and the winner is the one who finishes first.

Cars are designed to attract fans with bright colors and logos.

Drag racing began in the dry lakebeds of California and on military runways. There were no rails to keep **spectators** safe from out of control cars. There were also no **grandstands** for spectators to sit in and enjoy the race.

The spoiler on the back of the car decreases lift and increases fuel efficiency.

In 1951, Wally Parks started the National Hot Rod Association (NHRA). Indianapolis hosted the first national race in 1955. Now there are almost 150 NHRA approved tracks in the U.S. and Canada, each holding hundreds of events every year.

Wally Parks

Wally Parks, credited with starting organized drag racing, promoted safety at drag racing events.

Do you like cars? Drag racing involves over 200 classes, or types, of vehicles. The class depends on the type of car, engine size, weight, and **modifications** made to the car.

Top Fuel Dragsters

Top fuel cars move so fast that they have wings to keep them on the track. Two parachutes help them stop. **Nitromethane** instead of regular gasoline is used, and a specially built motor helps them go up to **330 mph (531 km/h)**.

Thrilling Fact

337.58 mph (543.28 km/h) is the fastest speed ever clocked.

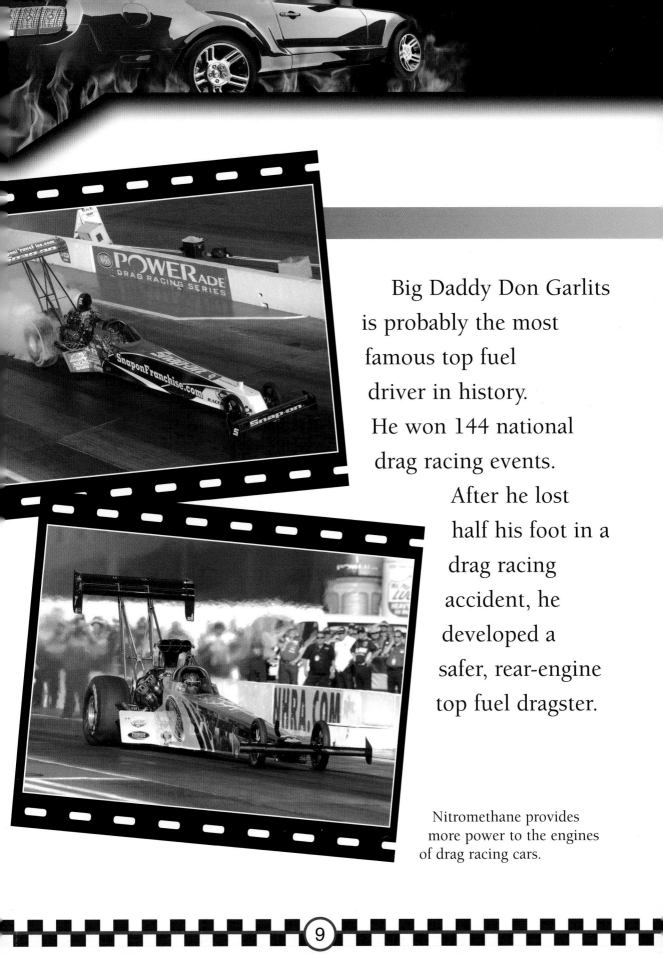

Big Daddy Don Garlits is probably the most famous top fuel driver in history. He won 144 national drag racing events. After he lost half his foot in a drag racing accident, he developed a safer, rear-engine top fuel dragster.

Nitromethane provides more power to the engines of drag racing cars.

Funny Cars

Funny cars also use nitromethane to help them reach speeds of up to 330 mph (531 km/h).

They have a big, rear **spoiler** across the back of the car that uses air to keep the car on the track. They are heavier and narrower than top fuel dragsters.

For Ashley Force, funny car drag racer, it is all in the family. She is the daughter of John Force, a 14-time NHRA funny car division champion. Both of her sisters also race. In 2007, Ashley made history by racing and beating her father.

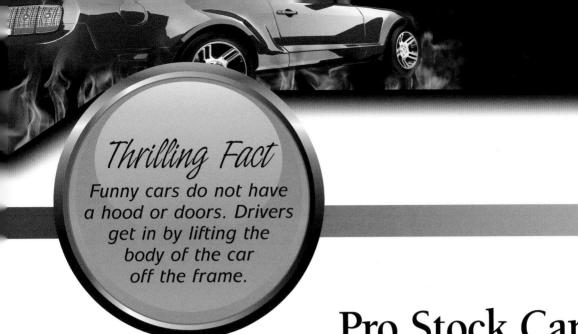

Pro Stock Cars

While these cars look a little like the cars your parents may drive, modifications make them drive much faster. They have two doors, a rear spoiler, and must be younger than five years.

Pro stock cars must weigh at least 2,350 pounds (1,065 kilograms) including the driver.

Super Street Cars

Picture your mom burning rubber as she races down the drag strip in her minivan. Don't laugh, if she wanted to, she could test her metal in the super street cars class. Super Streets include sports cars, vans, and panel trucks with fenders, hoods, grilles, tops, windshields, and working doors.

Almost anyone can race in super street cars.

Pro Stock Motorcycles

Bikers drag race too. A pro stock motorcycle division began in the 1980s. Some riders say racing a motorcycle feels the same as shooting out of a cannon at 190 mph (305.78 km/h).

Rules state that riders must always wear a helmet while racing.

Junior Dragsters

You do not have to wait until you grow up to drag race. In the junior dragster class, drivers can range between the agesof 8 to 17 years old. You do not need a license, but you do need to be a member of the Junior Drag Racing League.

Junior dragsters are half the size of top fuel dragsters and can go up to 85 mph (137 km/h).

Handicap Races

Some drag races are not about who goes the fastest. In these races, drivers estimate how fast they will drive. They write, or **dial-in**, on their window the time they think it will take them to get to the

finish line. If one car has a slower dial-in, they get a head start. Any car that goes faster than its dial-in gets a **red light**, or disqualified. The car whose **elapsed time** (e.t.) is the closest to its dial-in is the winner in these races.

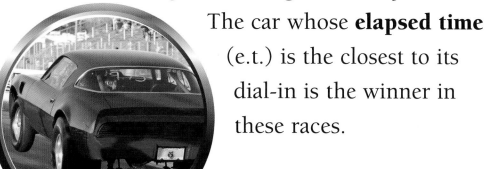

Drivers write their predicted
e.t. on their car windows.

If hurtling down a drag strip at more than 300 mph (483 km/h) sounds dangerous to you, you are right. However, drivers use special safety equipment. They wear a fire suit, with facemask, gloves, socks, and shoes. They also wear a crash helmet and neck **restraint**. Drag racers use a quick-release harness instead of a seatbelt.

A quick-release harness allows the driver to get out of danger fast.

Cars have safety features too. These include a fire extinguisher, damage-resistant fuel tank, roll cage, and bulletproof blankets wrapped around equipment that might break apart and hit the driver.

You probably live within driving distance of a drag racing track. These local tracks are a great place to watch all types of cars run. You can watch beat-up vans, pick-up trucks, and sports cars zoom down the track.

Races big and small attract fans across the country.

Big, televised drag racing events draw huge crowds. Some of the biggest include the Mac Tools U.S. Nationals in Indianapolis, Indiana, the Auto Club of Southern California, NHRA Finals in Pomona, California, the ACDelco NHRA Gatornationals in Florida, and the Carquest Auto Parts Winternationals in Pomona, California.

Show Me the Money

The cost of drag racing depends on the level of competition and speed of the cars. A hobby driver in a local race can pay $15 to $25 plus gate fee to race. Their car may cost about $25,000 to $30,000 and they can win up to $1,500.

Drivers have sponsors who help them pay for their cars and expenses. The sponsors use the car and uniforms to advertise.

The biggest races are a lot more expensive. Running a top fuel car can cost up to two million dollars per year including the car, truck, trailer, crew, and traveling expenses. The biggest prize is about $400,000, split between the driver and his crew.

Some people never outgrow the need to go faster. Other people are all about performance, building the best car and driving it as close to perfectly as they can. For these drivers and their spectators, drag racing is the best motorsport ever developed.

John Force and his daughter Ashley display winning smiles and a trophy.

Glossary

dial-in (DYE-uhl in): the time a driver estimates it will take to get to the finish line in a handicap race

elapsed time (i-LAPST time): the amount of time it takes for drivers to finish the race

instinct (IN-stingkt): an urge you are born with

grandstands (GRAND-stands): bleachers where people sit to watch the race

km/h (KAY EM AYCH): abbreviation for kilometers per hour

modifications (MOD-uh-fye-kay-shuhns): changes

mph (EM PEE AYCH): abbreviation for miles per hour

nitromethane (NYE-tro-meth-ane): a type of fuel made specifically for drag racing

spectators (SPEK-tay- turs): people who watch the races but do not race in them

spoiler (SPOIL-ur): a wing across the back of the car that uses air to keep the car on the track

reaction time (re-AK-shuhn time): how fast you begin moving after the green light

red light (RED lite): the light on the Christmas tree that shines when a car starts the race too early

restraint (ri-STRAYNT): a device used to hold something in place

Index

Websites to Visit

www.jrdrags.com/index.php

www.factmonster.com/ipka/A0768332

www.dmoz.org/sports/motorsports/Auto_Racing

http://jr.dragster.nhra.com

Further Reading

Gigliotti, Jim. *Hottest Dragsters and Funny Cars.*
    Enslow Publishers Incorporated, 2007.

Pitt, Matthew. *Drag Racing.* Scholastic Library
    Publishing, 2003.

About the Author

Nicki Clausen-Grace is an author and fourth grade teacher. She lives in Florida where they launch the first World of Outlaws event each year. While she has never driven on dirt, she does enjoy cruising along the beach with her husband Jeff, and two children, Brad and Alexandra.